Another Sunny Day In Hell

By Jack Bell

Order this book online at www.trafford.com
or email orders@trafford.com

Most Trafford titles are also available at major online book retailers.

Printed in the United States of America.

ISBN: 978-1-4269-8174-6 (sc)
ISBN: 978-1-4269-8175-3 (hc)
ISBN: 978-1-4269-8176-0 (e)

Library of Congress Control Number: 2011912832

Trafford rev. 07/29/2011

 www.trafford.com

North America & international
toll-free: 1 888 232 4444 (USA & Canada)
phone: 250 383 6864 ♦ fax: 812 355 4082

For Nina Marie
You are my Heart...

Thank you to my parents Jack and Mary Bell, my brothers Steve & Johnny, and to all my friends and family for putting up with my shit for all these years, you know who you are.

Also special thanks to Renee Hatten for all your help putting this book together and for the title page photo, Mark Pedemonte for the cover art and Barbie Avila for the back cover photo.

Table of Contents

Another Sunny Day in Hell

I open my front door and sit on my porch.
I light a cigarette like I have done hundreds of times
before.
The leaves on the trees have all fallen to the ground and
the trees are bare.
It is winter, but it is sunny and warm.
I think to myself that all this will be gone some day?
The houses and apartment buildings.
The street and the sidewalks and the streetlights.
All the cars and people.
I look south towards the beach.
Everything will be underwater from a flood.
I am only a quarter of a mile from the ocean's waves.
Or maybe underground from a huge earthquake.
Perhaps both.
I hope not in my daughter's lifetime, but I don't know?
Sooner or later Mother Nature takes it all back.
She's good like that.
I think of all the good and bad times I have had in this
apartment and on this street.
I am on house arrest.
My ankle bracelet mocks me.
I cannot go anywhere on such a beautiful, sunny, winter
day.
If I make it to March 25th I will have beaten the bracelet.
If I cave and go for a drink, it will beat me and I will go
back to jail.
Today, I will win.
Tomorrow is a new battle.
Just another sunny day in Hell......

8/14/1989

Tonight I went to a club with some friends.
I paid and went in.
I bought 3 shots of Jack Daniels,
Then 2 more Jack and Cokes,
Then a Tequila Sunrise.
I saw an older man lust after a bar maid.
A woman jealous of this blond girl.
I saw a band try *too* hard. I saw a couple *act* in love.
A very unoriginal place.
My friends did not want to stay.
I got bored.
I was uninterested in the scene.
I ordered another shot then left.
The bouncers were all fake.
The club was all fake.
There was nothing real.
There was nothing solid.
Nothing clean?
I went home.
Ate a piece of chicken.
Took some bong totes.
Then listened to The Doors 13
I am not supposed to drive until 10/10/89.
So I am stuck.
My room is not bad.
But it is small.
Oh well, I live on.
I hate driving.
But I hate walking more.
It is summer.
It is hot!
Tomorrow I must go to hypocrite school. (School Ten)
They think they are precocious.
But they are nothing.
I will smile tomorrow morning.
And be glad I am me.

Judas

My dog sings

WHOOOOOHOH-HA

My dog sings

One for Duane

I had a friend, a long time ago
We'd go to the bar and an occasional show
We'd get high on his blue bong
Talk and drink all night long
His VW bus would always break down
So we'd use my car to drive around town
He'd call on the phone and say "Whats up for tonight?"
Sometimes we'd get drunk and fight
Sometimes we wouldn't talk for a week or two
But we were always best friends, this is true
We'd go to the river, or Old Mexico
We'd go to the desert, or ski in the snow
We'd stay home on weekdays, go out on weekends
But through it all we were always best friends
He'd always share what ever he had
He was a true friend and for this I was glad
When he'd knock at my my door, I'd usually smile
And we'd sit and talk for a little while
We'd scrap our change together to buy some beer
I really miss him, I wish he was here.
We wasn't lucky with women, or lucky in life
His life had some turmoil, but he had strife
We'd get tickets together and laugh at the cops
We wouldn't leave when the party stops
I'm mad that God took him, & know that I'm wrong
All I can do now is write him this poem
I hold up my beer and take a big drink
My heart it is sad as I sit here and think
I really miss him, I know that he's gone
All I can do is write him this poem
I look to the sky and say good-bye to Duane
Life is so different it wont be the same
We'll never party again, or smoke from his bong
So all I can do is write him a song.

Bleed

Crucified ambitions
Of the moon
Loses strength
Before the dawn
The death screams tonight
Are unusually withdrawn
Through life's breath
Everything has gone
And your ambitions
Linger on,
and on
and on
Nailed to the cross
They are bled
But not lost.

I look out my window

I look out my window
The sky is grey
The winds blow the leaves to some unknown place
The trees look skinny and tangled with telephone wires
I wonder if the wind that blows outside is the breath of
some forgotten God?
Or maybe that when the wind blows the Earth is just
turning faster?
But I know it is untrue
To wonder

I look out my window
I see men building buildings we don't need
Working for a pocketful of nickels so he can buy some
beer and go back to his room
To take his family to McDonalds for dinner
To buy his wife something he cannot afford

To make payments on a car five years old already
If they work hard enough maybe they can build that
liquor store up so high they'll reach heaven and be saved
from all this shit
Even if they could do that they don't look like they have
the will
The skeleton of the building seems to be sucking the life
from them
Brave men

As I look out my window
There is no women here, no booze, no money
I don't feel so bad though because I have bottles filled with
air in the trash cans of my soul
My mind is filled with visions of her ribs tan in the midday
sun
I know the sun will rise again tomorrow
Somewhere there are cases of whiskey
Somewhere there is a vineyard with dew covered grapes

I know somewhere in St. Louis there is a brewery pumping
out Budweiser
I know that young girls grow older with every minute as
the older women count them
One or the other will be here in my room soon enough
So my solitude does not breed oppression
As I lay back on my bed and smile a thousand smiles
My remoteness a triumph
A small victory in my war
I'm getting closer
I can feel it in my bones
Victory

I look out my window
The sky is gray
The wind blows through the trees

Reality

Seeing through blind eye's
I see true reality
Feeling nothing
I know you do not care
Hear my words
Deaf to your ears
In this world
You can but live never
Try to help or give
That would be an error

Make something out of nothing
Nobody will care

In degree to destruction
Give your life
Toward the betterment
Of mankind

In the fires burn
Sell your soul
Burn with me in Hell
Lust devours all
Ecstasy and remorse
You ask your corpse
Dig, dig, dig, for your life
And you've dug your grave
Fuck living
Welcome to life
Burn for all to see
And fuck reality.

Highway 60

The road is wide open in front of me
Leading the way to your front door
Tires turning faster, engine breathing fire
Highway 60 is gonna get me to my girl
On the road nothings in my way
Never gonna stop, never turning back
Gotta drive, drive, drive

I Never Told Anybody This...

I met her on a hot, drunken Memorial Day weekend night in Parker, Arizona 15 years ago.

My friend had a house there that we were visiting and she was staying with her cousin at the camp grounds just down the road.

We hit it off immediately and spent pretty much the whole weekend together.

Drinking and fucking like it would never end.

When we got back to California I broke up with my girlfriend and she broke up with her boyfriend so we could be together.

We were in love.

I got her to move down from L.A. to Orange County and we got a little apartment together.

That only lasted about six months before she moved back to L.A.

We went back and forth to see each other trying to make it work for the next year and a half.

Mostly me going up there actually.

I would drive 50 miles just to have lunch with her for an hour, then drive back home.

In a very unoriginal desperate act I bought her a ring that she did not want.

I was blind and thought doing that would make it all better.

But it didn't.

In the end, she finally left me for her boss.

The owner of a company that made bongs and hash pipes.

He was married and his wife didn't think it was funny so she kicked him out.

The last time I talked to her he was hiding in the closet of the little apartment she had in the valley.

And she wanted to be with him.

I was devastated and crawled inside a bottle.

For the next decade it was an endless barrage of bars and women.

Booze roared down like an avalanche from a mountain.

Like a waterfall in Peru.

But there were no rainbows rising out of the mist at the bottom.

Only hangovers and depression.

The women I did not care about, because they were not her.

The one's that got close enough knew about her.

I don't know how though, because I never spoke of her?

Their questions fell on deaf ears.

They knew I was fucked up when they got on the train.

And those tracks lead to nowhere.

I must have thought about her a thousand times.

But I never told anybody.

I spoke to her on the phone the other day.

We hadn't talked in 13 years.

She sounded exactly the same.

She married her boss, but he cheated on her too.

They got divorced a few years back.

She has a new boyfriend now.

He is about the same age as I was when she left me.

She is coming over to see me this weekend.

But I don't feel sorry for the guy.

If I made it through losing her, he will too.

Some things never change?

Cum to me

Come to me
Just sitting at the
Bar
Hoping
Then it happens
Not sure but hoping
Then it happens
All the unoriginal
Assholes and me
Then you pick me
why?

Nina Marie

Well it took me awhile to realize
Very soon I'll look into your eye's
Your my little angel sent from up above
And from my heart and soul I give you all my love
I close my eye's and fantasize about you in my arms
About your birth, your stay on Earth, my little lucky
charm
I can't wait to hold your hand and see your little smile
Tuck you in bed and kiss your head and watch you sleep
awhile
I'll never love anything as much as I love you
For my little girl there's nothing I wont do
I would give you the world, but it's not mine to give
You will always have my love as long as you shall live
Your eye's bright, I'll hold you tight and never let go
I am glad that I'm you dad I just want you to know
All I do will always be for you Just you wait and see
I will always love you my little Nina Marie

As She Sleeps

As she sleeps with her head upon her pillow
My fingers gently brush her hair from her cheek.
Her face looks like that of an Angel, peaceful and beautiful.
She is content and warm, she knows with me there, she is safe.
What she dreams of, I do not know?
But I do know it is not of me.
I am so close to her, yet so far away.
As she sleeps I turn off the T.V. and blow out the candles.
Lock her door and close it behind me
Walk down the stairs and out to my truck.
As I sit there, I breathe a heavy sigh.
I wonder why I screwed things up so badly between us?
Drove her into the arms of another man?
I have no answer or excuse for myself.
As she sleeps I start my truck and drive into the night.
At home, I put my key in and open the door.
Go to my room and get into bed.
As I fall asleep in my bed alone
I think of her face, one last time.
I know what I will be dreaming of this night.
I will be dreaming of her.
Because I still love her.

False Notion

I had a notion
But it was false
Not gonna ride this feeling
Not gonna ride no more
For I obey me
Not gonna sit below
No one else's tree
I had a notion
But it was wrong
Not gonna think this way
Not gonna think no more
Not gonna obey you
Why cant you see?

Johnny Boy

I remember the day you were born
Dad drove Steve and I to that hospital in Anaheim
We were to young to go into the hospital to see you back
then
Dad took us to the side of the building where we climbed
through some bushes
On the other side was a big window
We looked through the window and that was the first
time I saw you
Mom looked really tired and her hair was all messed up
She was holding you in her arms
She was really happy with a big smile
You were all pink and blue
She said something but I couldn't hear her through the
glass
I looked at Steve and he was so close to the glass he was
fogging it up
She picked up your little arm made you wave to your two
new big brothers
I knew in my heart right then I would always love you
And though many years have gone by
And a lot of shit has happened
I still do

Unclean

The solemn look in your eye
Impaled with a stare
encompassed by time and you will feel so unclean

Why wont you just speak
you just hide or run away
But I will find you and we'll go another round

By the time you realize
the honest truth and open your eyes it will be far to late

Feel adrenalin pumping this time I'm going to win
I close my eye's. I'm jumping
I land in all my sin

Life is a test
To see how long it takes
For you to snap or lose control

Why don't you, why don't you
take a look around
you will see
I'm not lost your found

The wind does not care

I rode on a sparrows wing to a place that I cannot recall.
I fucked a Goddess three times in two different centuries.
I went to planets with no names.
I met two dozen people that I hated and got drunk on golden water.
I love my friends, the few.
I love my family.
I will miss them if I do not return.
The world is minute compared to the universe.
The crow is hated by the dove.
The wind does not care and it carries them both.

My Little Dented Can

As I smoke my last cigarette tonight at 3:09am
I think of you
My little dented can
I got you half of at the grocery store
Because you were damaged
You're blue eye's begging me to come over
Then asking me to leave before the sunrise
Because you're sugar daddy is in love with you
And you're boyfriend smacked you around
He cant satisfy you cause he's an idiot
I care about you, but could never love you
Just ain't gonna happen
Too many years in the bars fucked your head up
As I smoke my last cigarette
I think of you
My little dented can
Sweet dreams

The blank page

The blank Page
Why do you mock me?
Fuck you
Sometimes all the things I want to say don't come out
right
Now I know why everyone isn't a writer
Cause not everyone has balls.
Fuck You!

Chewy

The beginning of your life wasn't easy
I know this
I was there for a lot of it
But you did well
And worked hard
For that I am proud of you
You introduced my daughter and I to our extended family
You guy's know who you are
And for that I am grateful
You are a good man
And no one can ever take that away from you
Not even that selfish little bitch
You are a good Father, Uncle, and friend
And always will be
Cause that's the way you are
I wish I was
But I am not
Decades have gone by and I still think of you
When I am sad, fucked up, or alone
You always answer my call
For that I am indebted to you
You told me when we were teenagers
We would always be friends
That was a long time ago
It is 1:06 am
I am calling you
You answer
Standard issue

Right arm bro

Thanks For The Kid

I remember March 28th 1992 the day I met you.

I remember the phone number 984-7202.

I remember having lunch at E-Z Burger and feeding the sparrows french fries.

I remember listening to The Cult – Electric CD and hugging and kissing you for the first time.

I remember the ferris wheel in Balboa Beach and playing air hockey and taking pictures in a photo booth and you getting busted on the little boat ride there.

I remember your house on Oaks Ave. in Chino that first week we met.

I remember thinking that I'd never met anyone like you and how you made me feel.

I remember all the animals you had.

I remember feeding the horses hay and carrots.

I remember playing with the cats and dogs.

I remember going to the park and playing basketball.

I remember going to the carnival and dancing to the Mexican music.

I remember the dinners with your family.

I remember the good times and the bad.

I remember when you were happy and when you were sad.

I remember every time you cried and every time you let loose that gorgeous smile of yours.

I remember driving up your driveway and waiting for you to open your door.

I remember driving away while you stood outside your house waving goodbye to me.

I remember going home on the 60 freeway thinking I could hardly wait to see you again.

I remember sitting on your bed and hugging you real tight for five minutes without saying a word.

I remember my Mom and Dads 25th wedding anniversary and your beautiful blue dress.

I remember how proud I was to be with you that day.

I remember going to the beach.

I remember all the holidays.

I remember sitting in you house waiting for you to come home from the club.

I remember going to the movies with you to see Captain Ron.

I remember going grocery shopping and having dinner with you.

I remember waking up in the morning next to you and thinking how peaceful you looked as you slept.

I remember there was a ghost in your house.

I remember writing poems and songs for you and how sometimes you would like them so much you would cry.

I remember the day you told me you were pregnant.

I remember the concerned look in your eyes.

I remember those weren't the easiest days for either one of us.

I remember a lot of worrying.

I remember our first break up.

I remember the day our daughter was born.

I remember how proud I was when I held her.

I remember thinking that you were the most incredible woman I had ever met in my life.

I remember thinking that was the most important day in my life.

I will love that child till the day I die, and then after that, I will love her for eternity.

I remember all the stages of her growing.

I remember the first time I saw her smile.

I remember the first time I watched her alone.

I remember the first time she rolled over.

I remember the first time she sat up by herself.

I remember her first crawl, her first step, her first tooth, and her first word.

I remember your apartment on Center Ave.

I remember when you asked me if I wanted to get back together with you.
I remember feeling nervous, like a school kid that night.
I remember when you moved to Orange County and you stayed at my house.
I remember the time we went to Black Angus for dinner.
I remember taking our daughter to Discovery Zone.
I remember when you moved to Huntington Beach.
I remember how I felt when we broke up again.
I remember feeling really unsure about the future.
I also remember thinking some how it'll work out alright.
And it has.
I remember just about everything that we've done and been through over the years we've known each other.
Good and bad.
And I'll never forget any of it.
I remember yesterday and I remember today.
And I can't wait for tomorrow.
I remember the first thing I ever said to you that night at The Roxy in Hollywood.
I remember walking up to you and saying,"I think you are beautiful."
And that's the first thing I thought the first time I saw our daughter.

I Broke a Mirror

Cut my head on New Years Day
Beat my friends and beat myself
Stayed up late with my friend E.J.
We got nothin better to do
Ripped my shirt and started bleeding
But my blood will always dry
Stayed up late with my friend E.J.
Cause our friendship never dies
All I want is to lay down
In my bed and close my eyes
But my phone rings
And my brain will always sigh
You say, I say, we say
Nothing at all
I scream, you scream, we scream
I hear no call
Vacuum my rug but it's still dirty
 And so is my mind
Strain my eyes and stare at the sun
But it only makes me blind
Cut my head on New Years Day
Beat my friend and beat myself
Stayed up late with my friend E.J.
Cause we got nothing better to do.

What Should You Do?

Bunch
of
mother
fucking
hypocrites
around
you.
Spewing
their
shit
at you.
Telling
you
how
to
be.
What
should
you
do?

Inebriated

My father's beatings
unbridled
My toes under the rug
scratch
Feels good
but the way I feel is not
My daughter looks at me like I'm God when I catch a lizard
but I'm not
Beer bottles in the trash can
Friends
Who?
Starting again
Fighting
Concerts
Whiskey
Beer
Speed
Coke
Pot
Heroin – the best of all!!!
Sports
Jail – cops
Anger
Love
Fuck
God
Eternity
Nothing
Shes the best/worst girl on Earth
Hurt
Spite
Drunk
Loose canon?
Super asshole
Strong drink
Writer
Brazilian Jiu-jitsu
I want to learn how to take a man apart.

Enjoy Your Prime

Life is like an apple
It is born and it grows
In its prime
It shines like the sun
It is ripe
It lives.
But then gravity pulls it
From its providing Mother
And it falls.
Sitting
Waiting on the ground
It waits for someone to come
To come along and pick it up
If someone comes
it will be devoured
And its life will have been worth something
If no one comes
It sits and waits
And waits, and waits, and waits
Until it is no longer desirable
And then it rots
And rots, and rots, and rots
Until it is no longer red
But brown
Now no one wants it
So rotting
It sinks slowly into the ground
So enjoy your prime
For you will not always be desirable.

You Cannot Reach Me Now

You
cannot
reach
me
now.
Just
try
and
you
will
see.
You
cannot
teach
me
how.
Theres
not
much
left
of
me.

She Will Cry

The wind blows
Through the trees
And through my window
I feel the breeze
The sun shines
Bright and warm
One thousand miles away
Is the nearest storm

A lazy summer day
Holds my soul at bay
The sky is blue
Like her eyes
But my love
for her slowly dies
My heart is with
The sun and moon

My love is with
The stars and sky

My soul will be
leaving here soon

And when I go
She will cry

Out of Line

No one can beat you
Your fever gets higher
You never bothered to know
Spinners spinning
I need your love
But you give yourself away
I don't wanna die
But I don't care
Pray
Pray for me
Fuck the people
They will deny you
You've got to burn

Thoughts at 6:18

As I sit on my bed lighting my last cigarette.
I think about my past.
Some good, a lot of bad.
I enjoyed the party's, the friends.
The sunsets and sunrises drinking.
But I mostly enjoyed the women.
Smart ones, dumb ones, rich ones, poor ones.
Lunatics, angels, drunks, painters, waitresses.
Nurses, strippers, receptionists, models.
I have had fun with them all.
But I do not miss the arguing and fighting.
Right now I'm with a stripper.
She has a smile that lights up the sky in the middle of
the night.
And everything seems OK.
Living day to day.
Talking about things no one cares about but us in a little
house in Ontario, California.
She's tall and blond with golden eye's.
She drives slow and she loves animals and she loves sex.
But I don't like to throw the L word around too much.
She dances like a goddess and does well at the club.
When the sun is murdered by the night and darkness falls
upon the land.
Men get in their cars and drive to the club to watch her
dance.

All these men.
All different.
She's open and direct about her work.
Professional.
She seems truthful enough, sincere.
I don't mind her occupation, a jobs a job.
Sitting on my bed putting out my last cigarette.
I think about my present.
I wake up in the morning and I remember to breath.
I eat when I'm hungry and I sleep when I'm tired.
I have a gorgeous lover with a most intriguing personality.
I have a penny in each shoe so if I die they can put one on each eye.
I'm glad I'm with her.
I don't think about death or other negative things much anymore.
I try and think of good things and the future.
Cause it can get very, very dark alone.
Crouching in the back of your mind.
Knowing that something inside you.
Wound up like a clock.
Can never be wound again,
Once it stops.

Promises

The day's make promises they can not keep
Every day the lies are in the first ray's of light
Taking until night comes to expose the only truth
How many days?
When will we see the true light?
Minutes are centuries
As we live through the ages

Fuck the police

Stone cold faces that never smile
Lock you up cause of your lifestyle
Drinkin and drivin on a Friday night
Your turn to step into their spotlight

But this one's mine

Fuck the police

House Arrest

I sit here like an animal in a cage
I haven't left my apartment in days
No one to talk to
Nothing to do
I walk to the utility cabinet in my kitchen
Inside there is a box of size 16 nails
I open the box and take one out
It is long and shiny in the kitchen light - beautiful
I grab the hammer
It is night and raining outside
I sit on the cold floor
I look at my feet
The green veins run through them like tiny highways
Blood flowing in them keeping me alive
For some reason I think of Christ on the cross
I put the point of the nail on the center of my left foot
I see and feel the point as it pushes on my skin
I slam it through my foot with the hammer as hard as I
can
I feel the pain shoot from my foot to my knee
I hammer the nail all the way into the floor
I stand up and start skipping in circles
Going nowhere
Foot nailed to the floor
Like riding an imaginary skateboard
Round and round I go
Theres quite a bit of blood on the floor
I slip and fall
When I get up there are two bloody hand prints on the
linoleum
I skip in circles some more

Now the floor is covered in blood
I slip again
This time I cant get up
I just lay there
Bleeding out with my foot nailed to the floor
Looking up I see the ceiling fan
Turning and turning
Its still raining outside
I hear the rain on the window
Each time I blink it gets darker and darker
Then – black
I can barely hear the rain
Then – nothing
I awake in my bed to the alarm clock
It is 6:20am
Time to get up and get my daughter off to school
Sometimes in this life you just cant win

9/11/01

Today most heinous things were brought upon me
A dark hour
What I've seen on TV makes me sick
What I see can not be real
But it is
And forever will be

Unreliable

My love's like a roller coaster
It sounds like fun at first
Then when you get done
You feel like your gonna puke

I'll always be
dreaming of you

I have often told you stories about the way
I've lived the life of a dreamer waiting for the day
I could hold your hand and look in your eye's
And maybe you would say
That you will always love me and never go away

But now I feel I'm growing older
And the songs that I have sung
Echo in the distance
Like the sound of the world spinning round
I guess I'll always be dreaming of you

Many times I've traveled looking for something new
In the days of old the nights were cold
And I wandered without you
In those days I thought my eye's had seen you standing
near
Though love is confusing my heart was so sincere

But now I feel I'm growing older
And the songs that I have sung
Echo in the distance
Like the sound of the world spinning round
I guess I'll always be dreaming of you

Time to move on

Although we fucked and drank a thousand times
It's time to move on
Although we smoked and drank a thousand times
It's time to move on
That little girl had some lovin to give
But now it's time to move on
Blink your eyes and I'll be gone
Cause now it's time to move on

Love Is....

Love is like the sight of a lobster or crayfish
It knows not where its going
And only sees where its been.

Love is like eating corn on the cob made of wood
It leaves splinters in your gums.

Love is like a piece of shit
You don't know its there
Until its too late
Your in it.

Love is ice in Hell
Love is fire in Heaven.

Love is like a boat in a dried up sea
Its just there.

Love is endless amounts of beer.

Love is the reflection of a fire in her eyes.

Love always turns to lust
Love is lust with a vail
Love is lust in the shadows
Love is dark.

To be in love
Is to be blind.

To be in lust is infinite
The possibility's endless.

Love is darkness
No moon
No light.

Sea Of Madness

An infinite sea of madness
Is what we're cast into
A sea of deception and greed
A world with only you
There may be people you think you know
But in fact you really don't
The human race are worse than animals
Only because they know and realize what they do
Love is a feeling that turns to hate or fear
Very few people live happily together for many years
But on the other hand
Very few people live happily alone

My Friend

The Lord took my friend the other day.
And he didn't tell anyone of his plan.
I phone my friends house but he is gone.
What is the area code for heaven?
The Lord didn't want him to listen to Led Zeppelin with me anymore.
Or go to the beach.
Or take bong totes.
Or drink beers.
The Lord didn't want him to stay here with us.
I can never go to a concert.
Or to a party.
Or to Rockin Bowl.
Or to Jack in the Box.
Or to a liquor store with my friend again.
Maybe the Lord was jealous and just wanted to do these things with him himself?
At night when I am drunk I talk to my friend.
I wonder if he can hear or see me?
I wonder if he is laughing at me because I am acting like an ass?
I don't quite know but I feel him close every once and awhile and this is good.
He knows my area code and my phone number.
He knows where I live and I feel him drop by sometimes.
Late at night when I'm in bed I hear the clapping of flip flops on his heels.
I smile as I fall asleep because I know he is near.
The Lord took my friend away the other day.
Good-bye my friend I will never forget you.
Someday I will see you again.
But for now, I will take a bonger and raise my drink to you.
For a full minute.

It's Been Awhile

It's been awhile
Since I last saw you
And I know now
That we're not through

These days alone
Were happy days
But not the same
Without your ways

Don't know why
I felt that way
So with you
I'll have to stay

To Not Feel Thankful

FUCK OH FUCK OH FUCK OH FUCK
FEEL LIKE I'M OUT OF LUCK
BUT I KNOW I'M REALLY NOT
I'M JUST NOT THANKFUL FOR WHAT I GOT
FUCK OH FUCK OH FUCK OH FUCK
FEELIN LIKE I'M FUCKIN STUCK
BUT I KNOW I'M REALLY NOT
I'M JUST NOT THANKFUL FOR WHAT I GOT

FUCK OH FUCK OH FUCK OH FUCK
I HAVE BEEN RUNNING AMUCK
I'M NOT THANKFUL FOR WHAT I GOT
PLEASE JUST GIVE ME ANOTHER SHOT
FUCK OH FUCK OH FUCK OH FUCK
DRINK & FIGHT & SPIT & CUSS
CHILDREN DONT GROW UP LIKE US
PISS OH SHIT OH FUCK OH NO
WAITIN FOR THE BOOZE TO FLOW
PISS OH FUCK OH DAMN OH SHIT
GET MOTHER FUCKIN BLITZED ON IT

The Sights Of My Burned Out Mind

I hate this

I hate this

I don't like
the feeling

My skin
is peeling

I don't like
growing old

I don't want
my life to fold

Everything
was going well

Until I fell to Hell

These are the sites
of my burned out mind

It's All In Your Mind

Don't want to think about you
No I don't wanna think no more
Don't know what I'm gonna do
When I picture you walk out the door
Because its all in your mind
Think I'll go out and party
I'll have myself a ball
Don't need your animosity
Don't need to answer your call
Because its all in your mind
Don't want to think about it
Don't want to think it again
Don't need your shallow shit
I'll get myself another friend
Because its all in your mind
Don't want to hear why you don't care
I don't need to know
You're just another girl out of my hair
The only fan at your show
Because its all in your mind

The Cult

John woke me worried about Bemo's ticket.

We went to Prissy's Choice Tickets and got it on will call.

We drank a twelve pack of beer at John's house.

I went home and took a shower.

I went back to John's and we drank more beer.

Bemo drove his Pinto with John.

I drove my Volkswagen with Steve and Danny.

We drank a bottle of Bacardi and another twelve pack of beer at Twin Lakes Park

We got kicked out of the park for being loud.

22 freeway to the 5 freeway exit Irvine Center Dr.

Stop at Circle K for more beer.

We arrived in the Irvine Meadows parking lot at 7:00pm

The Cult didn't start until 10pm

We drank, and drank, and drank.

John punched Danny in the eye.

I met a girl named Liz.

We all went in to see The Cult.

I pissed my pants a little waiting in the SUPER long line at the restrooms because I was drunk.

The Cult put on a good show.

After the show we got in a fight with some amateur drunks in the parking lot.

John passed out in Bemo's Pinto.

The remaining four of us continued to drink.

We finally left the parking lot at 1:15am

And this is good......

My last real day with Jill

I drove my car to her house. As I walked up to her door
her cats followed me.
I knocked.
Jill answered and let us all in.

She had just finished cooking something in the kitchen.

We sat and talked at the table. Afterwards we went into
her bedroom and got stoned.
We laid on her bed holding each other sensing the end.
We both smiled, we hugged, kissed.

Will you rub my hands?

No. I replied.

We laid there, didn't fuck, just laid there holding each
other.

Will you rub my feet?

No. I said.

She had her paintings on the wall,
 posters of Picasso, and some other pictures.

Her cats liked me more than her.

Her room is always messy and her ceiling is pink.

Tell you what. Get me a pen and I'll draw that Picasso
poster on your foot. I said.
She got a pen quickly.

She loves when I rub or massage her neck, back, back of her head, shoulders, arms, hands, butt, legs, and feet. Especially her hands or feet. I grabbed her right foot and within 20 minutes I had a pretty good version of Picasso on it.

We talked some more about a few things I don't remember

Maybe we should see other people? We could still go out, but also see other people. I said.

I'm pretty sure we both already had someone in mind.

But me and you could still go out. Right? She said.

Yes. I said.

Now everyone knows you cant have a relationship with someone and go out with others without making the other person jealous.

Thats where we fell.
Jack & Jill R.I.P.
February 1985 – December 1989

We both laid there on her bed. Holding each other.
Smiling.
Thinking we were pretty damn smart,
but we weren't.

A lack of good

There is something

Something that I lack

Wont you tell me

Is what I lack, good?

Seasons

I love women in the summer and winter. This is my romantic, sexual time. Like I said, my time. I am selfish with my time. Therefore I give two seasons to women and two seasons to myself. To me women are not yearly. They go by seasons, attitudes, thoughts, totally mental. I need time alone and usually they take it the wrong way. It is neither of our faults, but then again, what the fuck?

Women of Summer:
Goddesses. Especially California women. No matter how dark their hair it is always lightened by the sun. No matter how light their skin it is always darkened by the sun. High energy, abounding joy, parties, sweating during sex, getting drunk outside at 1am with only a t-shirt and shorts on, holding hands, going to the beach, driving with the windows down, Watching David Letterman even though you have to go to work in the morning, smoking joints of skunk weed. Ah, Summer. Tan lines, Tanned smiles, young vitality, prominent girls ready to begin life, rambunctious older women feeling young, ready, both ready. I love it! The beach, inland bars, clubs, houses, beautiful. Yes, Summer is radiant!

Women of Fall:
I don't know? I really don't know? I seem to let myself go and fall. I usually get lost in the season. I usually break up with my girlfriends in Fall. I don't know why? I blame it on the season. I like to write in the Fall. It is a pattern in my life and I don't know why? Since I am writing about women, I'm not going into it any further. I love Fall. I have never had a serious relationship in Fall Soon I probably will, but don't count on it.

Women of Winter:
Cool, but not cold. Ever looking for warmth. I like that, because I have it to spare, to give. I smile better in the dark. Christmas cuts my throat and I bleed, smiling.

Catch me during this time and you have me till spring. I create my own horoscope. Girls who go by horoscopes are easiest. I usually have long hair in Winter because I think it keeps me warmer. I hate the holidays. Having a woman is comforting but expensive. I like days when it rains. Staying inside and being warm. I could never live in a place where it is cold all the time. It would fuck my system up. I like to burn candles over empty Jack Daniels bottles. Turn out the lights and burn candles and make love. That's great! Intimate. I am drunk now. I love blonds! I love Winter! I also don't think I can get married, ever.

Women of Spring:
Theres a myth that everyone fucks during Spring? People fuck all year round. Spring is the best time for me to write. To work. To keep busy. The women will come. Spring is a wonderful time of year. I usually get rid of the women from Winter at this time to prepare for Summer. I meet as many women as I can in Spring and call them in Summer. Spring is trans lucid and willing. The last stepping stone to Summer. I guess all I think about in Spring is Summer's next! Spring is over rated.
Like I said, I love women, I have all their albums.

The Addicted Undead

As I walk down the moonlit sidewalk the shadows from the trees look wicked as they dance in the wind. Zombies have been trekking paths toward this church I have almost come upon. Across the street the field is full. All walking my way. Why this place? I was very scared for I learned somehow that a bite from one of these undead creatures would transform you into one of them. Knowing this I was careful to avoid the slow moving zombies. Curious to see why they moved toward this old church I silently moved down the sidewalk. Running in and out of the decaying party. I found no reason for the gathering only to rest their evil souls to the alter and die? As if to redeem them for being undead. These zombies were not trying to bite, but warned of the others. The others were the addicts who had died on drugs. Feeding on the dealers and fiends. Showing no mercy and accepting what they find. The addicted undead. No one was safe. A horrible chill was in me. I desperately thought I must do something. Suddenly a girl ran to me telling me crystal meth was the cure. The antidote for the bites. As she fell and was eaten before my eye's..........

Morally Debased

Corruption, oh sweet, corruption
Live and learn in hell then burn
Try to live they'll pull you down
18 years old 6 feet underground
Mom and Dad shed a tear
Blame it on all your peers
Why did we let him leave
No more parental pet peeve
Fuck all, fuck all
Ride the wind
Corruption, corruption
Live in sin how can I win
I'm morally debased
What can I say
I live my life day to day
Futures a myth can it be faced
By someone morally debased?

Yes.

I am the future.

Until I am the past.

Crossing Ellis

I'm heading south fast
Don't know how long it will last
You put this feeling in me
Nothing but pain and animosity
Your lies cut me like a knife
Every day of my life
Going to see the only joy I know
Faster, south I go

And now I'm crossing Ellis
Looking left all the way
And now I'm crossing Ellis
I know I've got to pay
And now I'm crossing Ellis
Gotta face the bad to get the good
And now I'm crossing Ellis
Just like I knew I would

So unstable and insecure
So manipulating and I'm pure
I love my baby and that is why
I look into your cold uncaring eyes
If not for her you'd be a distant memory
Your not so special don;t you see
Thats why people treat you the way they do
When you lie the truth is coming through

Me, Pammy and a bottle of J.D.

Thursday afternoon as the sun drops behind the purple smoggy mountains I talk to Pammy smoking a cigarette. "Let's get a bottle and get drunk tonight. Then fuck like racehorses." I said.
She didn't say anything, just smiled.
We went to Albertsons and got a bottle of Jack Daniels, a sixer of Coke, and some Hostess cherry fruit pies.
We came home and got comfortable.
I made the drinks.
We sat on the couch with the c.d. player on watching t.v. with the sound turned down.
We drank and smoked and talked.
I love talking to Pammy because she is so real.
She's not stuck on anything.
I couldn't resist anymore.
I leaned over and we kissed.
We kissed and rolled around on the sofa for half an hour.
Then we went upstairs.
That night I had some of the best sex I've ever had in my life.
When we were done the bed sheets were so wet we had to put new one's on so we could sleep.
We kissed and said goodnight.
When the lights went off I laid there and thought, "What am I doing here with this beautiful woman, drunk at 4:14am, 33 miles from home with a quarter tank of gas and $2.38 in my pocket?"
Then I remembered our sex marathon and thought, "Who cares, I'd be a fool not to be here!"
Good night my love......

Well into my phase

It has begun no regret
My phase is set
Drink, smoke, live
Never, never, never give
Well into my phase
Give no ground
Impale you with my gaze
Your body will never be found
Death – Irrelevant
Mind – Gone
Eyes – Piercing
Hands – So strong
It has arrived I thrived
On my phase
Drink, smoke, live
Never, never, never give
Well into night
Darkness, oh sweet, darkness
Bring me home tonight
Cause my phase has arrived

Burning Desire

Corruptions here, this evil sphere
Wicked world turns with fear
Hell awaits, with open gates
It just gets worse with every passing year

Societies desire, sets man on fire
Everyones calling the mirror a liar
Living dead, God turns his head
As the cities flames reach higher

And fucken higher

I smile better in the dark

That little girl makes me feel blacker than the darkest night.
She makes me think things I should not think.
Sin runs through my body but I do not care.
I watch her eyes, her body, her hair.
When the lights go out her eyes glow
She makes me hot, she gets me high, all I see is black.
I turn her over and forget about my world.
I feel darkest when I'm with that little girl.
18 years old but I gotta laugh.
Dont even think about what could happen to me?
Sin runs through my veins I do not care.
Her eyes meet up with my stare.
I watch her eyes, her body, her hair.
I blink my eyes 3 times and she was never even really there?

Feel My Pain

I feel like I'm about to lose my head
I feel like I'm rotting away
Just laying on my bed
I feel like I'm doing just as best that I can
But what can make me feel
Like a ordinary man

My mind is not solid, I have no control

Now I know I don't know everything
But everything is a bit much to take in
And there may be someone out there
Who may not agree
But he ain't writing poems
So you have to listen to me

My mind is not blooming, I have no control

I feel like writing a novel
I feel like I'm in love
But still theres something wrong
I feel like I cant take anymore
But it's hard to leave
When you cant find the door

My mind is decaying, what is control?

Am I just being deceived
Or are these people fucking me
I tell you now I just don't know
All you people out there
Please tell me
Is it yes or is it no

My mind is empty, fill it with a soul

Well I'll tell you right now

I cant take too much more of this
My mind is all covered
In a great foggy mist
As my eye's begin to roll
My feelings take their toll

My mind is gone, there is nothing left

If you don't like me I'll just crawl inside
And if you don't like it I'll just run and hide
Inside your brain
Don't worry you'll just go insane
I'll look through your window when it hurts
Then you'll feel my pain

Why?

Why do I feel this way?
Thinkin too much or maybe not enough
Really don't know
Which way I gotta go
Havin trouble with a decision
That I must make
Do I give or must I take
Really don't know
I'm feelin kinda down
Feel a little blue
Don't know what im gonna do

Gotta leave so why do I stay
Feel like kickin but I go away
Where am I going
Don't really know
I write right now
But got nothing to say

Feel my heartache
My mind is just there
Don't know why I feel this way
And now I don't even care

Niggardly

She reaches so high
She stoops so low
She starts to cry
She don't even know
She wants it all
She don't want to try
She doesn't call
She don't know why?
She says she love's me
She says she's scared
She says she's not free
She said she cared
She said she quit smoking
She says her car don't run
She said she was joking
She doesn't like to have fun
She wants a lot of money
She dances late at night
She says she's busy
She says she has no time
She says she's dizzy
She's in her prime
She's not faking
She's 6 I'm 9
She is taken
She's mine, all mine.

The guy that's not me

There is a guy and he's not me
He is a person being someone he cannot be
There is a person who wont leave me alone
There is a guy in me I guess he is my clone
Doing things I shouldn't do
Putting me through things I shouldn't go through
Listen to me, ya I'm talking to you
Two people, one body, to me this is new
When I am drunk, he is there
When I am sober, my brain we share
When I am eating, his tastes seem fine
When I am sleeping, his dreams are mine
There is a guy hes in my head
I think that he'll be there until I'm dead
I know that he is me and I am him
I know that I alone do not make two
So why the hell am I talking to you?

So why the hell am I talking to you?

Hammerhead

He's got a girlfriend that goes real fast
He's got a life, but it wont last
Past out drunk at 3am
Got up at 6 to do it again
People say he should slow down
Or he'll end up underground
10 minutes to 2 gotta get some beer
He would drive but he cant steer

He rolled his car for a DUI
Woke up outside and he don't know why?
Counts his change to get some booze
No way to win, no way to lose
We gotta go to the liquor store
We're outta beer and need some more
Will smoke a joint without fail
Go in the bathroom and do a rail

You'll never die
You can't deny
Goin all the way
Each and every day
Ain't go no women but he's got wine
Half way through the label and feelin fine
Gets so wasted that he cant see
So am I talkin bout you or me?

To Be Alone

Arms outstretched, but no ones is there.
Hug and grasp at ice cold air.
What do you see when you look into my eyes?
Feel my emptiness, hear my cries.
Something is in my mind.
But I just don't know what it is?
Something I was hoping to find.
But I don't know what it is?
I reach out, the illusion is you.
Just like a mirage, I reach out to you.
Arms outstretched, theres nothing there.
Nothing but invisible air.
Disappear before my eye's.
Feel my emptiness, hear my cries.
Without saying my last goodbye's.
My illusion of you slowly dies
And again...
I am alone.

Evil

Evil is a friend of mine
To me he is quite the kind
The kind that don't follow a rule
If you don't look like a fool
Evil is the party's spark
Evil is light in the dark
Evil backwards is the opposite of death
Evil till my last breath
Evil is black and white
Evil is always right
Evil is usually corrupt
Evil is always abrupt
Hang from the roots of an oak
And in sin your soul shall soak
Evil is eternity
Evil in you
Evil in me
Cant escape
No you cant hide
Evil is the horse I ride

Disenchanted Emperor

I try so hard to keep myself cool
But I find it so hard when they look at you
So I get into fights
And you start to cry
I look in your eyes
You'll never know the reason why

So here I sit empty and alone
A disenchanted emperor
On a lonely throne.

Everyday I think of you

Everyday I think of you
The way you smile and things you do
You are not just my baby, your my best friend
And I will love to the very end
Your so special, you mean the world to me
We watch the birds flying over the tree's
Cant bare the thought of not seeing you
Little Nina, your daddy loves you
You can't talk, but I know you know
That your daddy loves you so
Your my princess, my shining star
You will be, no matter where you are
You are my only bright spot in a world gone mad
And I'm so proud to be your Dad
When I carry you in my arms
You will be safe, there will never be harm
I'd give my life for you my little one
Your smile shines brighter then a thousand suns
There's magic dancing in your eye's
That's something money can't buy
I pray your face never shows a frown
I promise I will never let you down
Everyday I think of you
And always know that your Daddy loves you

Little Black Thing

Little black thing that lives under my couch
Why do you take my things?
First a pair of sunglasses
Then one of my women's shirts
Now a book I was only half way through reading
And where are Chewy's keys?

Little black thing that lives under my couch
I have called all my friends and none of them have my
things?
I saw you one night when I was looking for them under
there
When you closed your eye's you disappeared
Are you under there wearing my shades
Wearing my womans shirt and reading my book?

Little black thing that lives under my couch
I want my things back
You little fucker!

Gimme back my Bukowski book!
I talk to you late at night when I am drunk
I try to make you feel better
Because I know how lonely it can be
But you continue to take my things
At least put my book back on the coffee table
So I can finish reading it
Then you can have it back

Little black thing that lives under my couch
I accept you
At the end of the day
When the sun goes down
I know you are there
And it comforts me when I am alone
Because you are insane
Just like me.

I Forgot

Today I forgot how to breathe
And I forgot just what I need
I saw the world laid out before me
I saw everything so small
If I think, I think of you
If I think, I think of you
I scream at the sky, her eyes are bluer than you
I felt so bad I almost forgot all about you
I forgot how to cry
And I forgot I could die
And I'm so sick of what I need
Slit my wrist but I don't bleed
If I think, I think of you
If I think, I think of you
I open my eyes, watch the sky turn blue
I felt so good I almost forgot all about you

Cause I'm Sick

Staring out the window
Start of another day
I love to be all alone
But they don't go away

Going to go out and talk to my dog
Then I'll feed him the cat
Go out and get high on the smog
Till I don't know where I'm at

I want to make a jail break
But theres no escape from my mind
Everything around me seems so fake
I'm so ahead, but I'm so behind

Think I'll watch the sunset
So I can wait for it to rise
I know I promised, but I forget
So there not really lies

Wanna jump into your eye's
Are your colors all the same
It would not be a surprise
Cause your all so fuckin lame

Blitzed

Kickin back
Wanna hit the sack
But I don't know
If im going back
Don't know where to go
I love these friends
I have gathered
To stay and party
I would have rathered
But now I know
Where to go

But I'll be back.

Gaul

The colors drive me insane
Wanna play in the acid rain
I am hurt but I feel no pain
No gain

Got a picture in my head
I am living among the dead
In place of dying I sleep instead
Shread

My key ring has an extra key
Don't have a cage but I'm not free
My sight is fine but I can't see
Who's me

Blood on the rug, on the bed, on the wall
Gotta run, gotta walk, gotta crawl
Took a little, took a lot, took it all
Gaul

My tongue is like a razor
Gotta lick just to shave my face
I'm a speeding trailblazer
Gotta get out of this place

The Street

When I look out my window what do I see?
The sun, the sky, the grass, the trees
The street lays silently, but is wise
Many a thing has it seen with it's eye's
Many a thing has it heard with it's ear's
Some happiness, sorrows, joy, and tears
But as I look out of my window on this afternoon
The night will crawl over the day very soon
And as the moon comes to put all to sleep
The dark will take over and into it I leap

To All My Peers

The lives of others I do appall

Soft white underbellies, no arms, no legs

They crawl, crawl, crawl

I may mingle, but I'm not them

Visionary, I ascend

I am my one and only friend

Boundless, lost forever

Like blind lost sheep

Into their pionic minds

Do I like to creep

The orientation of their life

My tongue cuts through them like a knife

Exhaust all knowledge through their ears

And expose them to all their peers

Invalid lies revealed to me

As I burn their family tree

My quintessence is my soul

It's the only thing I have that is immortal

Everyone must live within themselves

And not in others pitiful health

I've learned a lot in all my years

So, fuck you, to all my peers!

Sometimes

Sometimes I'm happy, sometimes I'm sad
Sometimes I am good, sometimes I am bad
Sometimes I sleep, sometimes I don't
Sometimes I do it, sometimes I wont
Tried it all with a smile
Been on top of the shit pile
Seen people come and people go
I'm so smart, but I don't know?

I did the line of fire
Going fast I will not tire
Speeding right through the night
Thinking I'm wrong, but I'm right

Come on and take a ride with me
Got the key to set you free
Wanna help you cleanse your soul
Rake the embers over the coals

Running fast to stand still
Looking for the next thrill
Don't want it all I just want some
Don't know where I'm coming from

Sometimes

The Deep End

When I go to the deep end
I piss out large amounts of beer
When I go to the deep end
I piss out vast amounts of beer
I feel good
As I should
I feel
I know its wise
Theres no disguise
Descend down with fire
Lifts my soul higher
I'm a man
We're obsolete
I judge
How I should treat
Real
Is how I feel
And I feel
Like descending

Down
Down
Down
Down

Down to the deep end

Forever.....

Nothing lasts forever
But we like to think so in our minds
No, it wont last forever
If you think so you are blind
There was a day not so long ago
When I thought love would last
But little did I know

We had lots of good times
I felt it in my heart
No they weren't all bad times
And yes it was a start
Although I still love you
And your a million miles away
Don't be sad, no dont be blue
You know this is what I say

If you think of me remember
That I love you so
Just close your eyes and I'll be there
But this you already know
I've been with other girls
But none of them like you
I've got you in my dreams
And I know you love me too
I will love you until I die
Then there it will end
With my last good-bye
My long lost lonely friend

Free

I've been thinking about you a lot lately
All the things we used to do
Time has been moving oh so quickly
So many things that we've been both been through
Many times we watched the sun go down
And a few times we even saw it
rise
I always felt good lying next to you
Hope our love for each other never dies
I helped you through times that weren't so good
And in turn you did the same for me
I held you tightly in my arms
And when I let go you were free

Thanks

You were always there for me
Even when I didn't see
How wrong I really was

You always gave me love
And the chance to rise above
Without a hesitation or a pause

Major Tweekage

I hit the ground hard today
But I didn't feel it at the time
Tried to talk but had nothing to say
I sure was feelin fine

I believe one can only go so far
Gotta really believe in who you are
Take it to the limit, take it to the sky
Now thats the reason you get high

Party animal the times you had
Way back then you didn't feel so bad
Now you've found your life's mistake
Feel your body start to ache

I sure was feelin good
But I didn't know where I was at the time
Tried to talk as best I could
It was home I had to find

Or is it?

Highway 5

Drive drunk down Highway 5
Pick up my girl and drive, drive, drive
Cruise through the city of sin
Modern day Babylon, city of sin
Traffics high the lights are bright
I drive down Highway 5 into the night
Black night the moon's cold stare
Shines light on the path we share
As we drive our destinations not there
But we don't even care
Drive drunk down Highway 5
Into the fucked up night
Alright

To Mold Myself For Whatever?

I feel great animosity towards myself
Not enough books on my shelf
I want to be alone, but I am lonely
I want to be silent, but I am heard
I want to go away, so why do I stay?
Why do I live my life this way?
Oh, why do I live my life this way?

My vocabulary sucks, so I cant say
Oh well, I'll read the dictionary another day
My pen writes down my silent thought
So wound up, my nerves are taught
Capillaries tied within a knot
The booze make my eye's bloodshot
All my life for this I've fought
Why do I live my life this way?
Oh, why do I live this way?

I want a girl who cannot speak
I want to mold her to be meek
My fingers shape her body line
To me this would be so sublime
But even if I did this, with time
She would develop her own mind
Then I'd leave her far behind
But I would not leave her till after her prime
To me this would be so sublime
Why do I live my life this way?
Oh, why do I live my life this way?
Why do I live my life in affray?

Fuck if I know?
I laugh with madness

Powers of Observation

Illusions of a time are always on my mind
The ones who have followed and the ones I have to find
But through it all I've learned to crawl
To wherever there is light
I hate to say there may be a day
That I lose my sight

We are prisoners of our minds
Reminding us it's time
Darkness is always what we fear
Cause in the light we see so clear

Colors of a place you see every day
But when darkness falls you are open prey
Whispers in the wind
Say our minds are thin
Watch close but see not a thing

The powers in my head and I'll see through what you
said
It's in your eye so please don't lie
As you lay down on your bed
Remember me and you will see
The powers of observation
Are what will set me free

The Show

Standing here
This atmosphere
A place that I call home
I look around
What do I see
One thousand people roam

Drinks in hand
We see the band
Deep vibrations set us free
As I stand
And watch the band
That sing these words at me

All These Things

All these things within my head
And all these things that I have said
Mean nothing until I find the light

All these people around me
I wish they could see
Their ways to me aren't right

If I could do what I want to
I would fly away to the sun
The things I say I think all day
But none of them I've done

The vibration of strings to me life brings
But the power is not in my hands
And the things that are true if I knew what to do
As I wake thats when my brain lands

I wish I could go far away
Far away towards the stars
But im stuck here every day
I feel like I'm stuck behind bars

But in the end I'll never bend
And everything will be alright
When I touch that star which ain't very far
Then I will be my own friend

Sinking

I give you all my love
And all you give is shit
I tried my best to save you
But your sinking quick

You don't like when I smoke pot
And you frown when I drink
You tried your best to save me
But cement shoes will make you sink

Gotta know, gotta need, I want your touch
That's alright it ain't worth that much
I am what I am you wont change me
What you get is what you see

We're sinking down
Cant tread much longer
But it's not too late
I'm not holding my breath

Feeling Sublime

Waiting for warm beer
Waiting for it to get cold
They sell it cheaper when its warm
But cold, as much as gold
Tax the liquor, tax the smokes
As congress crack their jokes
Normal folks don't get a rest
The government is such a pest
County jail or state pen
You're your one and only friend
So think not of the people who are high
Cause to you they wouldn't even bat an eye
Live your life as you are
Cause no one's gonna fight your war
Get "key buy" whiskey and buy warm beer
Take it home and have good cheer
Save a nickel, save a dime
For some gas to get to work on time
My poem is done and so is my brew
It sure was nice talkin to you
But these words were just to pass the time
Till my beer got cold, now I feel sublime

Looking Around

looking around at everything

this fuckin town, the things I've seen

so burned out on this scene

looking around at everything

need a change, but I don't know

covers over my head suffocating slow

bunch of dead heads think their cool

not knowing their the joker

not knowing their the fool

Joe

JOE TWEKELING
DID NOT CARE
THAT THE GIRLS
LAUGHED AT HIS HAIR

A SINGLE BUTT HAIR

Veneration

WOKE UP THIS MORNING
WITH A CLOUD AROUND MY HEAD
A DAY IS BORN
AND I AM DEAD

Sleep

Life is cruel with it's twists and turns
Life goes on and sometimes burns
Life in general ain't what it seems
I like it better in my dreams

Innocence and Experience

A day of this, a day of that
The innocent they slowly learn
An hour, a day, a month, or years
The innocent they slowly learn
Theres a big difference
Between innocence and experience
One becomes the other
and the others extreme
After its over and you already know
The years they slowly burn
As you grow old and try to think
The years they slowly burn

Time

Transplexed in meaningless effort
Dying to live for the sun
Hearing winter die, cold and alone
A friend and pen is all I have
Time is of the essence
Time will always tell
Good or bad it will be heard
Months to years
Hours to days
Speak

Stillborn

Walking lonely down a lonely street
Sorrowful drunkenness bellows in my mind
I see a suicides game taking a stride
Horrors die all our wars inside
Sinking dead from our worlds end
Shall the worlds collide
Bringing down a subtle taste of annihilation
Before our kind darkness